# Cocker Spaniel Coloring Book

## By

## Feel Happy Colouring

# Want To Feel Happy?

Well you are in the right place – we are called Feel Happy Colouring Books after all!

Feel Happy Colouring are a group of talented artists that share a passion for creating fun and relaxing coloring books. We aim to help you switch off from the outside world and unleash your inner child, passion and creativity.

Please do write to us and give us your feedback, we genuinely would love to hear from you. What coloring books would you like us to do next?

Our email is help@feelhappybooks.com

We also want to post your finished artwork on our own website and Facebook page so share it with the world if you dare...

www.feelhappybooks.com

www.facebook.com/feelhappybooks

# Copyright and Trademarks

For comments, questions, requests for review copies and bulk order discounts please also email:

help@feelhappybooks.com

ISBN: 978-1-910677-32-2

# For Best Results...

1. Use this page to test your markers and pens before you start on a real picture.

2. We do recommend you put a sheet of paper or card behind each page for the ultimate protection of each page below it in case of bleed through.

3. With each picture printed on one side of the page only, it means you can remove your finished artwork and frame or display proudly without losing the picture on the other side of the page.

4. Don't feel you have to start from the first picture. Feel free to color in any way you wish, there is no right or wrong way.

5. Reduce noise and distractions, coloring can be a great time to relax and activate your imagination.

6. Above all - have fun!

## CAN WE PLEASE ASK A SMALL FAVOR?

Please consider helping us by 'paying it forward' – posting a positive review really does help us reach more people.

Most people don't realise this, but the more reviews we get, the higher our book gets shown on online book retailers and adds more credibility for undecided buyers so it REALLY is important.

Leaving comments is really simple and quick, please go to the book retailer, find our book, scroll down to the bottom of the page and click where it says 'write a review.'

If you feel we can improve our books, please contact us directly as opposed to leaving permanent comments online. We are more than willing to change and improve any of our pages.

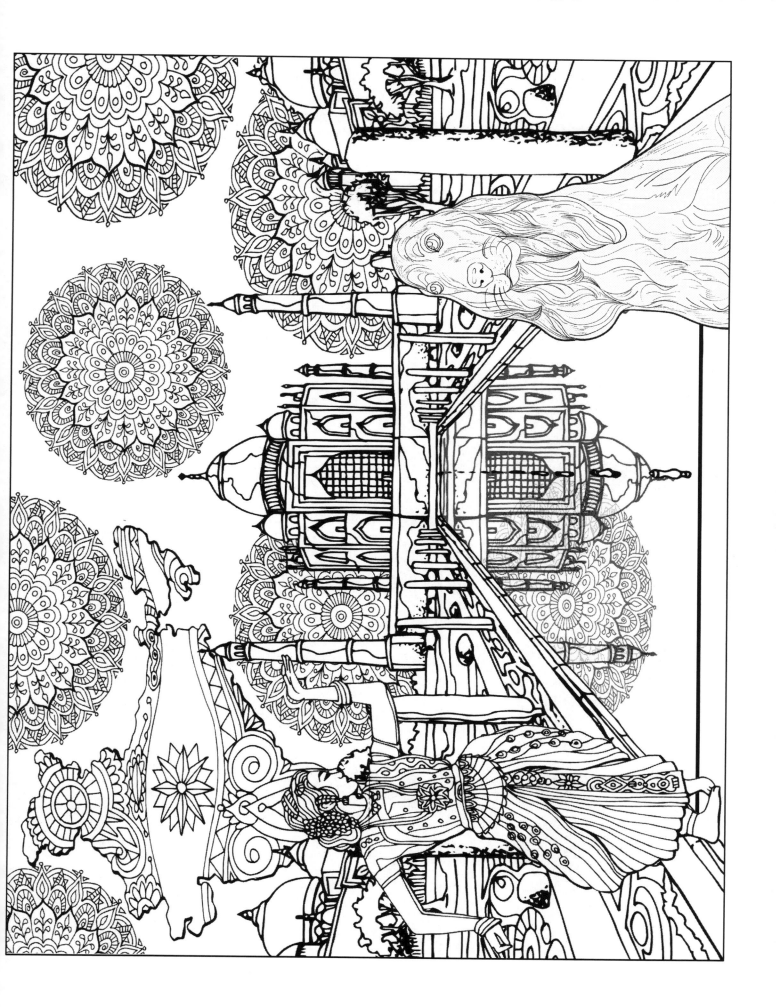

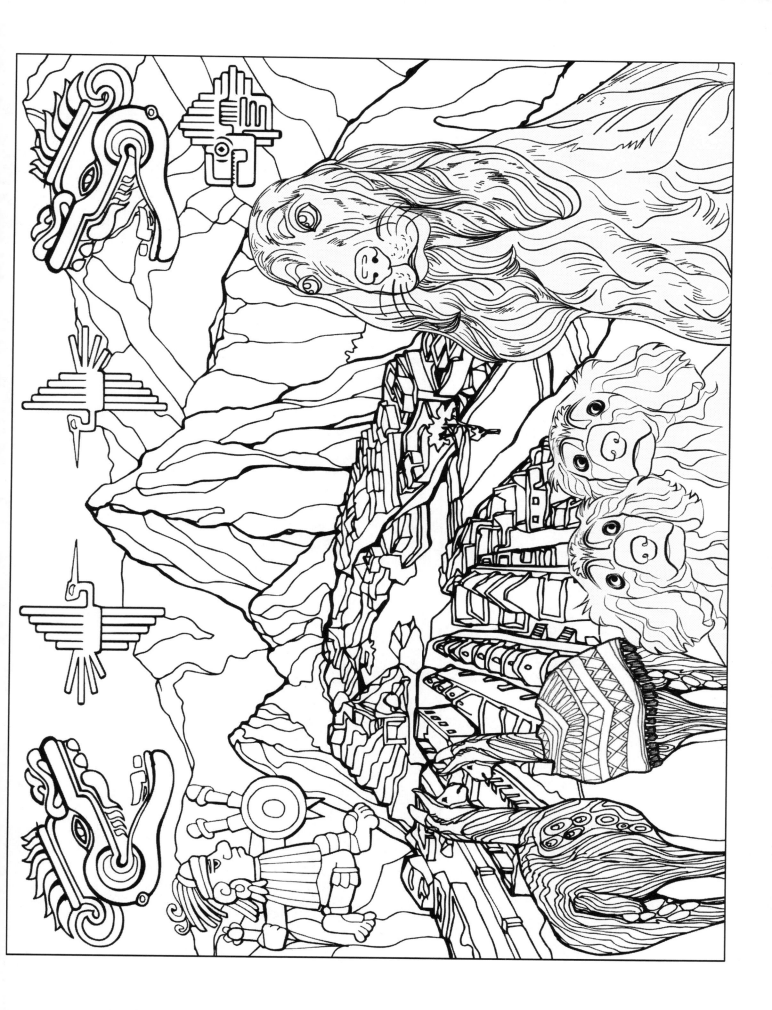

# GET THE FREE BONUS EBOOK...

We want to say thank you for purchasing this book and to give you a special surprise. To show our appreciation, we have a **free e-book that you can download (and then print)** consisting of 10 sample pages from some of our other coloring books.

Thank you once again. To get the free book, just go to the web page below and follow the instructions. If you have any issues or feedback/comments, please send an email to help@feelhappybooks.com

www.feelhappybooks.com/secret/

## We Love Reviews

Positive reviews really do help us reach more people as they help get the book shown even higher up <u>and</u> add more credibility for undecided buyers, please help us by posting a review. Go to the online retailer where you bought this book from, find our book and click on 'write a review.'

If you have any comments to help us improve the book, then we would love to hear them personally and we can then revise the book as necessary. This is far more constructive than leaving a potentially harmful review.

## Thank You

We just want to say a big THANK YOU from all of us at Feel Happy Colouring for buying this book, we really do appreciate it so much.

# Gift Ideas

As well as other dog coloring books we have cats too and they make great gifts for friends and family. Just search for FEEL HAPPY COLOURING to find us. Here are just a small selection of our other titles…

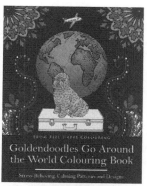

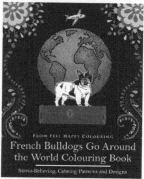

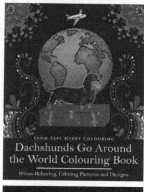

Made in the USA
Columbia, SC
28 April 2020